The
Asparagus Festival
Cookbook

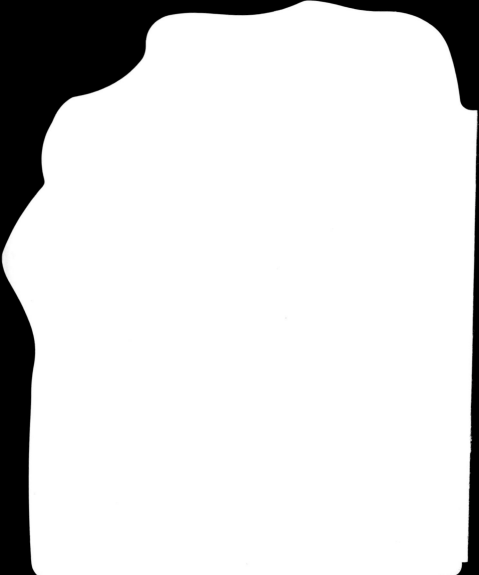

The Asparagus Festival Cookbook

by Jan Moore, Barbara Hafley,
Glenda Hushaw & Jacqueline Zupo

CELESTIALARTS

Berkeley, California

CELESTIAL ARTS PUBLISHING
P.O. Box 7123
Berkeley, California 94707

Cover Photo: Covello Photography
Cover and text design: Brad Greene
Printed in Singapore

Library of Congress Cataloging–in–Publication Data

The Asparagus Festival Cookbook / Jan Moore . . . [et al.].
       p.   cm.
     Recipes from the Stockton Asparagus Festival, Stockton, Calif.
     ISBN 0-89087-829-3
     1. Cookery (Asparagus) I. Moore, Jan, 1941–   . II. Stockton
Asparagus Festival (Calif.)
TX803.A8A87 1997
641.6'531—dc20   96-42091
                                                          CIP

First Printing, 1997

1 2 3 4 / 00 99 98 97

Contents

If ever a vegetable deserved a cult following, it is asparagus! Poets have sung the song of asparagus; artists have painted it; craftsmen have recreated it; photographers have captured it; healers have prescribed it; epicures have sighed over it; and kings have been inspired by it!

When Stockton, California decided to launch a festival to support community projects, charitable groups, and service organizations, asparagus—the "Rolls Royce of the Vegetables"—was the most likely choice as Stockton sits in the heart of asparagus country. Stockton hosted its first Asparagus Festival in

1986 at the beautiful Oak Grove Regional Park. The three day event, always held on the fourth weekend in April, attracts some 100,000 asparagus lovers and soon-to-be converts.

Highlighting the Festival is the big-top tent dubbed "Asparagus Alley" where gourmet asparagus dishes are prepared to delight Festival goers. Featured in this cookbook are favorites like Deep Fried Asparagus (literally tons of asparagus are used), Asparagus Bisque (sheer ambrosia), and Asparagus Pasta (perfect for pasta lovers).

Other recipes are tried and true winners from previous Recipe Contest Cook-Offs and the Asparagus Country Fair—including everything from delicious lasagna to foods for the "I don't eat asparagus crowd" like tempting pickles, jelly, guacamole, salsa, and even sweet desserts! The poppy seed loaf, sherry cake, and

Waste Not, Want Not Cake are all something to enjoy!

What other vegetable is as much a delight to eat as it is healthy for you? Asparagus contains significant amounts of vitamins C and B_6, thiamine and potassium, has more folacin per serving than any other vegetable, and is high in fiber and low in salt too! All the recipes here are guaranteed to please your palate and help you on your way to good health. Cook, eat, and savor the wonderful way of asparagus!

Measuring Asparagus

APPROXIMATE NUMBER OF SPEARS
IN ONE POUND OF ASPARAGUS

Colossal Size	7 or fewer stalks not < 1" in diameter
Jumbo	7-10 stalks not < 13/16" in diameter
Large	11-20 stalks not < 7/16" in diameter
Standard	21-30 stalks not < 5/16" in diameter
Small	31-45 stalks not < 3/16" in diameter

Diameter is measured at the point 9" down from tip

FRESH ASPARAGUS YIELDS

1 pound, trimmed	2 cups, cut up
1 pound, trimmed	four 1/2 cup servings, cooked
1-1 1/2 pounds	1 pint, frozen
2 1/2-4 pounds	1 quart, canned
2 cups, chopped	1 cup puree

PROCESSED ASPARAGUS YIELDS

1 quart, frozen	2 cups, grated
1 10-ounce package	1 1/4 cups, cut up
1 14-ounce can	1 1/3 cups, cut up

Stalking the Asparagus

All recipes require cleaned and trimmed asparagus.

Stockton Aparagus Festival Deep Fried Asparagus

1/2 cup cornstarch
3/4 cup flour
1 tsp. each salt and baking powder
1/4 tsp. black pepper
1/2 tsp. each white pepper, celery salt, and baking soda
2 egg whites
2/3 cup cold, flat beer
3 lbs. asparagus trimmed to 8 inches
peanut oil

Mix all ingredients except asparagus and oil in a bowl with a wire whisk until well blended. Dip asparagus individually in the batter and deep-fry them in at least 2 inches of peanut oil for 2 minutes or until golden brown.

Serves 6

Asparadillas

8 oz. cream cheese, softened
¼ cup mayonnaise
1 Tbsp. prepared mustard
10 fajita-sized flour tortillas
2 Tbsp. toasted sesame seeds
20 thin deli slices ham
30 thin asparagus spears,
    blanched and cooled
10 thin strips each red bell pepper
    and yellow bell pepper

Combine cream cheese, mayonnaise, and mustard in a small bowl. Divide mixture evenly between the tortillas, then spread to cover. Sprinkle ½ tsp. sesame seeds on each tortilla and cover with 2 ham slices. Place asparagus spear on edge of tortilla and begin to roll tightly, adding a red and yellow pepper strip and two more asparagus spears as you go. Roll tortilla completely and fasten with toothpicks. Finish all tortillas in same manner. Cut tortillas into 1-inch pieces to look like pinwheels. Discard ends.

Yield: 50 appetizers

Best Ever
Asparagus Dip

        ¾ cup canned asparagus,
            drained and mashed (fresh cooked
            asparagus may be used)
        4 chopped green onions including tops
        5 cooked and crumbled slices bacon
        1 tsp. dill weed
        1 pkg. ranch dip mix
        1 cup each mayonnaise and sour cream

Combine all ingredients, mixing well. Chill.
Garnishing with asparagus tips is optional.
Serve on crackers or as a vegetable dip.

Yield: Approximately 3 cups

Asparagus à la Rebecca

9 green onions including tops
8 cups diagonally sliced fresh
   asparagus
Vegetable oil for frying
2 cups fresh parsley florets
5 large eggs
¾ cups each Italian style bread
   crumbs and grated parmesan
   cheese
Salt to taste

Slice green onions lengthwise into quarters;
then into 1-inch pieces. Place in large bowl.
Sauté asparagus in oil until limp (use oil spar-
ingly). Add asparagus to onions, then add
parsley and eggs. Mix well. Add bread crumbs,
cheese, and salt. Mix well.

Heat oil in frying pan until quite hot. Shape heaping tablespoon of asparagus mixture with fingers while on the spoon so asparagus and onions mostly lay in same direction. Place in hot pan, keeping individual patties separate. Fry until brown, then carefully turn to fry other side. After turning, press down to flatten. When done, drain patties on paper towels.

Serve patties hot, room temperature, or cold. Can be served as a side dish or as an appetizer. Wonderful on top of thinly sliced French bread.

Yield: Approximately 48 3-3½-inch patties

Asparagus Paradise

¾ lb. asparagus cut into 1-inch pieces
6 green onions, white part only,
   thinly sliced
1 Tbsp. chopped shallot
4 Tbsp. butter
½ lb. grated Gruyère cheese
3 eggs
2 Tbsp. each chopped fresh mint,
   chopped fresh parsley, chopped
   fresh chives, and lemon juice
4 Tbsp. chopped fresh dill
1 Tbsp. salt
½ tsp. each white pepper and
   paprika
Dash cayenne pepper
1 cup butter, melted
12 leaves of phyllo pastry, thawed

Blanch asparagus in boiling water for 3 minutes. Drain, pat dry, and place in bowl.

Sauté green onions and shallots in 4 Tbsp. butter until transparent. Add to the asparagus.

Add cheese, eggs, mint, parsley,
chives, lemon juice, dill, salt, white
pepper, paprika, and cayenne pepper,
mixing well.

Preheat oven to 350°F.

Butter a cookie sheet with melted butter.
Lay 1 leaf of phyllo on work surface, and
brush with melted butter. Continue this process until there are 6 phyllo layers.

Place half the asparagus mixture along the
short end of the phyllo stack. Tuck ends in,
then roll up jelly-roll fashion. Place on a large
baking sheet seam side down. Make a second
roll with the remaining phyllo, butter, and
filling. Place on the baking sheet, leaving
ample space between the rolls. Brush rolls
with remaining melted butter.

Bake for 40-45 minutes or until golden brown.
Cool slightly, then slice into bite-size portions.

Asparagus Tidbits

3 oz. cream cheese, softened
Prepared horseradish to taste
8 thin slices ham, smoked turkey
    or dried beef
8 cooked asparagus spears
    trimmed to fit meat

Combine cream cheese with horseradish. Evenly divide mixture among meat slices, spreading on lower third of each slice. Place asparagus spear on top of the mixture at the edge of the slice; roll in jelly-roll fashion. Chill until quite firm. Cut into bite-size pieces, securing each with toothpick. Arrange on platter, garnish and serve.

Yield: 24 pieces

Asparazingers

4 medium eggs
1 cup low fat cottage cheese
¼ cup flour
1 tsp. baking powder
2 Tbsp. canola oil
½ lb. bacon, cooked crisp then crumbled
¾ cup cooked asparagus, cut into
    ¼-inch pieces
2 oz. chopped green chilies
1 cup grated Monterey Jack cheese
Salt and white pepper to taste

Preheat oven to 350°F.

Spray miniature muffin pans with Pam; set aside. In food processor, blend eggs briefly and add cottage cheese. Pulse to blend. Add flour, baking powder, and oil; blend. Stir in bacon, asparagus, chilies, and cheese. Add salt and pepper. Spoon mixture into muffin pans. Bake for 20 minutes. Let cool slightly before serving.

To serve, place zingers on a bed of finely shredded red cabbage or finely shredded lettuce.

Asparagus Seafood Almond Spread

1 lb. fresh asparagus, cooked and
  finely chopped
12 oz. cream cheese, softened
1½ cups ground almonds
¾ lb. fresh crab or shrimp meat
¾ cup mayonnaise
6 Tbsp. white wine or sherry
2 cloves garlic, pressed
2 tsp. prepared mustard
Finely chopped onion, to taste
Salt and pepper to taste

Combine all ingredients together and mix well. Refrigerate mixture for several hours to allow flavors to blend.

Spread mixture on baguettes or crackers as a cold hors d'oeuvre or heat through to serve as a warm dip with crackers.

Yield: Approximately 6 cups

Asparagus
Onion Dip

    16 oz. sour cream
    1 pkg. Lipton onion soup mix
    6 asparagus spears, cooked,
       blended to paste

Mix all ingredients together and chill.
Serve with chips and crackers.

Yield: Approximately 2 cups

Delicious Delta Delights in Croustades

CROUSTADES

1½ loaves sourdough bread
1 cup butter or olive oil
Garlic cloves, peeled and mashed,
  to taste

FILLING

3 Tbsp. butter
2 Tbsp. minced parsley
1 Tbsp. each minced shallots and
  minced fresh basil
1 lb. asparagus, minced and blanched
¼ cup minced fresh mushrooms
1 Tbsp. flour
¼ cup Madeira wine
1 cup heavy cream
Grated Gruyère cheese to taste
Salt, white pepper, lemon juice, dried
  thyme, and nutmeg to taste

Preheat oven to 375°F.

Croustades: Slice the bread, then cut into 2-2½-inch rounds using a cookie cutter or wine glass. Melt butter or olive oil in a small skillet with the mashed garlic until garlic gives off aroma. Roll out the bread rounds with a rolling pin. Brush the bread and the cups of a mini muffin tin with the mixture, then press bread into the cups. Bake for 10-15 minutes.

Filling: Melt the butter in a skillet. Add parsley, shallots, basil, asparagus, and mushrooms. Sauté for 2 minutes. Add flour and stir for 2 more minutes. Add the wine and cream, then simmer until the sauce is thickened. Add the cheese, salt, white pepper, lemon juice, thyme, and nutmeg. Fill the croustades. Place croustades on a cookie sheet and broil until cheese melts.

Yield: Approximately 60 croustades

Asparagus is low in salt, so it is ideal for a low sodium diet.

Asparagus is very low in calories. There are only four calories per spear, or 66 calories per pound. Great for the weight watcher.

Asparagus is outstanding as a source of rutin, important for keeping the capillary walls pliable.

Asparagus is rich in folacin, a B vitamin which helps duplicate cells for growth, repair the body, and reproduce blood cells in the bone marrow.

Folacin has also been found to be effective in the prevention of two of the most common birth defects, spina bifida and anencephaly.

One pound of asparagus serves from two to four people, depending on their appetite for asparagus.

'Gras Clippings and Soups

All recipes require cleaned and trimmed asparagus.

Warm Oriental Asparagus Slaw

SALAD

    1 lb. cooked and coarsely shredded
       fresh asparagus
    2 cups each shredded red cabbage and
       shredded napa cabbage
    1/4 cup each diced red onion, diced water
       chestnuts, chopped roasted peanuts, and
       chopped cilantro
    Black sesame seeds for garnish

DRESSING

    3 Tbsp. vegetable oil
    1 Tbsp. each sesame oil, soy sauce, sea-
       soned rice wine vinegar, and dry sherry
    1 clove garlic, pressed

Mix all salad ingredients except sesame seeds together in a salad bowl.

Heat dressing ingredients until hot. Pour the hot dressing over the salad and toss well. Garnish with sesame seeds and serve immediately.

Serves 6

California
Asparagus Salad

1/4 cup olive oil
1/2 cup seasoned rice vinegar
Juice of 1/2 lime
1/2 tsp. ground cumin
1/4 tsp. each oregano, black pepper,
  and salt
1 1/4 lbs. fresh asparagus
3 boned, skinned, and cooked chicken
  breasts, cut into bite-size chunks
  (other firm white meat may be sub-
  stituted)
3/4 cup mayonnaise
1/2 tsp. curry powder
6-8 large tomatoes
Lettuce for garnish

Combine oil, vinegar, and lime juice. Add
cumin, oregano, black pepper, and salt. Blend
well; set aside.

Reserve 2-3 inches of asparagus tips, then
slice the rest diagonally into 1/2-inch pieces.
Cook until tender but crisp; rinse with ice
water; drain well.

Combine sliced asparagus, chicken, and oil mixture to coat evenly; marinate for 8-10 hours in refrigerator.

Combine mayonnaise and curry powder; mix well and refrigerate.

When ready to serve, core tomatoes making an 8-point star by cutting from the top of tomato almost to the bottom, but not completely through. Open tomato into a flower (smaller tomatoes may be scooped out to form a bowl).

Line individual serving plates with lettuce leaves. Place tomato on lettuce, then fill each tomato with asparagus mixture. Top with curried mayonnaise. Garnish mayonnaise with reserved asparagus tips.

Serves 6-8

Technicolor Salad with Asparagus

DRESSING

1/2 cup olive oil
1/4 cup each walnut oil and raspberry
  vinegar
1/4 tsp. dry mustard
Salt and pepper to taste

SALAD

2 lbs. asparagus cut into 1 to 1 1/2-inch pieces
1 red bell pepper, seeded and sliced
  lengthwise into narrow strips
2 cups yellow pear tomatoes, sliced in
  half lengthwise
1/4 medium head red cabbage, sliced
  lengthwise, 1/4-inch wide
1 small head cauliflower, broken into florets
2 carrots, thinly sliced diagonally
1 cup sliced fresh mushrooms
3 1/2 oz. can sliced black olives, drained
1 head red leaf lettuce
1/2 lemon, juice only

Mix all dressing ingredients; set aside.

Steam asparagus until tender but crisp; chill.

Combine all vegetables except red leaf lettuce in a large mixing bowl. Toss gently with lemon juice. Add dressing to taste.

Line salad bowl or individual salad plates with lettuce leaves. Place salad on top of leaves.

Serves 8 as dinner salad or 4 as main dish

Fresh Asparagus Couscous Salad

DRESSING

1 clove garlic, very finely chopped
6 scallions, white parts only, finely chopped
   (reserve greens for salad)
6 Tbsp. lime juice
1 tsp. salt
Freshly ground black pepper
¼ cup vegetable oil
3 Tbsp. chopped fresh dill

SALAD

1 cup finely chopped onion
2 Tbsp. vegetable oil
2 cups each fish or chicken stock, water,
   and couscous
3 lbs. asparagus sliced diagonally into
   ⅓-inch slices; reserve tips
1⅓ cups radishes cut in half from top to
   bottom, then cut into ¼-inch slices
reserved green scallion tops, thinly sliced
   diagonally
1 lb. cooked small shrimp

In a small bowl mix the garlic, scallions, lime juice, salt, and pepper. Set aside.

In a medium saucepan sauté the onions in oil over medium heat for about 4 minutes. Add the stock and water. Bring to a boil, then stir in the couscous, remove from heat, and cover. After 5 minutes, fluff with a fork and allow to stand 5 more minutes, then fluff again. Transfer to a large dish and refrigerate. As other ingredients are readied, remove and fluff every 10 minutes.

Blanch the asparagus until tender but crisp. Place into iced water for 2 minutes, drain and set on towels to absorb extra moisture

Whip the oil into dressing with a fork, then stir in the dill. Mix the asparagus, radishes, green onions, shrimp, and dressing into the couscous. Serve over a lettuce leaf base, garnishing with the asparagus tips.

Serves 8

Asparagus and Fennel Salad

9 oz. fennel bulb cut diagonally
3 oz. proscuitto sliced and cut in
  julienne
4 Tbsp. olive oil
1 pinch white pepper
2 tsp. each salt and balsamic vinegar
1 pinch garlic powder
16 blanched asparagus spears cut
  on diagonal
1 lb. roma tomatoes, each cut into
  8 pieces
1 Tbsp. fresh basil cut into thin strips
8 oz. feta cheese, broken into small
  pieces

Sauté fennel and proscuitto in 2 Tbsp. olive oil until fennel is tender; add pepper and set aside.

Combine 2 Tbsp. olive oil, salt, vinegar, and garlic powder in a small bowl. Add fennel mixture, asparagus, tomatoes, and basil. Top with cheese.

Serves 4-6

Bella
Asparagus

2 lbs. large asparagus spears
1/2 cup olive oil
3 tsp. wine vinegar
1/4 tsp. garlic powder
1 tsp. parsley flakes
Salt and pepper to taste
6 chopped hard-boiled eggs
6 Tbsp. bacon bits

Steam asparagus until tender but crisp and drain.

Make dressing with oil, vinegar, garlic powder, parsley flakes, salt, and pepper.

While asparagus is hot, layer half the spears in a deep dish. Sprinkle on half the eggs, bacon bits, and dressing. Make a second layer of asparagus spears and top with the remaining eggs, bacon bits, and dressing. Serve at room temperature or chill.

Serves 4-6

Light & Fresh
Asparagus Soup

6 cups chicken stock
2 cups scallions sliced diagonally
(reserve 1/2 cup green tops)
1 1/2 lbs. asparagus sliced into 1/4-inch
rounds; reserve tips
3 Tbsp. lemon juice
1/3 cup cream or sour cream
1 1/2 tsp. finely chopped fresh mint
Pinch of cayenne pepper

Bring chicken stock to a boil in a medium-large sauce pan; add 1 1/2 cups scallions and cook 10 minutes. Add the sliced asparagus stalks. Bring the soup back to a boil and simmer 5 minutes, then remove from heat.

While the soup simmers, bring one cup water to boil in a small saucepan. Cook the asparagus tips for 3 minutes; drain and refresh in cold water. Slice tips thinly; set aside.

Purée chicken stock mixture in small batches using a blender or food processor. Return to the saucepan and reheat. Add the lemon juice, cream, mint, pepper, asparagus tips, and reserved scallion tops. Lower the heat and stir well—do not boil.

Serve hot or cold. Soup may be garnished with equal parts yogurt and sour cream, or topped with an asparagus tip.

Serves 8

Stockton Asparagus Festival Bisque

1/2 cup butter
3/4 cup flour
2 quarts whole milk
1 cup chicken stock (made from
    bouillon cube)
1 bay leaf
1 tsp. each white pepper and salt
3 cups cooked asparagus cut into
    1/2-inch pieces
Instant potatoes (use to thicken
    bisque if needed)

In stockpot, melt butter; add flour, stirring constantly so mixture doesn't burn. Add 1 quart milk slowly to roux, stirring constantly. When combined and thickened, add remaining milk and chicken stock. Add bay leaf, pepper, salt, and asparagus and cook slowly for 1 hour.

To serve, top bisque with large sourdough croutons and a spoonful of sour cream.

Yield: 1 gallon

Jan's Favorite
Asparagus Soup

3 chopped onions*
1/2 cup butter or margarine*
1 gallon water*
4 beef bouillon cubes (or more to taste)ᵏ
1-2 lbs. asparagus sliced diagonally into
   1/8-inch pieces
Grated jack or Parmesan cheese to garnish

Sauté onions in butter until they just begin to brown. Add water and bouillon cubes. Bring to a boil; add asparagus and cook about 3 minutes until it is barely tender. Serve with or without garnish.

ᵏ May substitute onion soup mix for these ingredients

Serves 6-8

Asparagus is a member of the lily family and has been cultivated for at least 2,500 years.

Approximately 25% of California's fresh market asparagus is exported, the largest markets being Japan and Switzerland.

Asparagus is available in United States markets nearly year around. California's San Joaquin County is the largest fresh asparagus producing county in the United States. Although we cultivate much of our asparagus here, imports also come in from Mexico, Peru, and Chile, among other countries.

California harvests asparagus many months out of the year. In southern California, the season runs from January through April, central California from February through June, and in coastal areas it is from July through October—all depending on the weather. A single field may be cut as many as 70-75 times each season—a number which is again dependent upon the weather.

Asparagus Front and Center

All recipes require cleaned and trimmed asparagus.

Stockton Asparagus Festival Pasta

1 cup each sliced fresh mushrooms
1/2 cup each chopped green onions
4 cloves garlic, minced
1/3 cup olive oil
1/2 cup olive wedges
1 cup diced fresh or canned tomatoes,
    drained well
2 cups cooked asparagus cut into
    1-inch pieces
1 Tbsp. each Italian seasoning and salt
1 tsp. pepper
1/2 cup marsala wine
1 1/2 cup chicken stock
Cornstarch wash (equal amounts
    cornstarch and water)
16 oz. fusilli pasta, cooked and
    drained
Grated Romano cheese

Over high heat, sauté the mushrooms, green onions, and garlic in the oil until tender. Add the olives and tomatoes. Heat thoroughly. Add asparagus and dry spices, stirring constantly. Add marsala wine to deglaze, then add chicken stock. Add cornstarch wash to thicken to desired consistency. Pour over pasta, mix, sprinkle with cheese, and serve hot.

Serves 6

Shrimp, Asparagus and Fresh Herb Linguine

12 oz. linguine
7 Tbsp. unsalted butter
3 Tbsp. olive oil
1 lb. cleaned medium raw shrimp
8 garlic cloves, minced
1/3 cup chopped shallots
2/3 cup bottled clam juice
1/2 cup dry white wine
1/2 cup chopped fresh parsley
1/4 cup chopped fresh dill or 1 Tbsp.
   dried dillweed
1 tsp. pepper
Salt to taste
1 1/2 lbs. cooked asparagus cut into
   1-inch pieces

Cook linguine until just tender. Drain pasta and return to same pot to keep warm. Mix in 1 Tbsp. butter (reserve the rest).

Heat olive oil in heavy large skillet over medium heat. Add shrimp and sauté about 3 minutes, stirring frequently. Using slotted spoon, transfer shrimp to a bowl. Add garlic, shallots, and 1 Tbsp. butter to skillet. Cook 2 minutes, then add clam juice and wine. Increase heat and boil mixture about 8 minutes, until reduced by half. Reduce heat to medium-low. Whisk in remaining butter. Return shrimp and any accumulated juices to the skillet. Add parsley, dill, pepper, salt and linguine; toss to blend well. Add asparagus and toss gently to mix.

Serve 4-6

Asparastrata
Kassandra

1 finely chopped onion
4 cups thinly sliced asparagus, cut
  diagonally
6 cups 1-inch cubed white bread
2 cups each shredded cheddar cheese
  and shredded jack cheese
7 eggs
2 1/2 cups milk
2 tsp. each salt and paprika
1/2 tsp. each pepper, garlic powder,
  and dry mustard
1 tsp. oregano

Mix onion, asparagus, bread, 1 cup cheddar
cheese, and 1 cup jack cheese in a bowl
(reserve rest of cheese). Set aside.

Combine the eggs, milk, salt, paprika, pepper,
garlic powder, dry mustard, and oregano,
mixing well. Add to asparagus mixture and
mix well.

Pour mixture into 9 x 13-inch dish sprayed with Pam. Top with remaining cheddar and jack cheeses. Bake at 350°F for 1 hour, or until golden brown. Let rest for 10 minutes before serving.

Serves 12 as a brunch or lunch dish, 15 as a side dish.

San Joaquin Valley
Enchiladas

2-3 lbs. fresh asparagus cut into
  1-inch pieces
12 tortillas
1/2 cup oil
1/2 cup each butter and flour
3-4 cups chicken broth
1 cup sour cream
1/2 cup green taco sauce
3 cups grated jack cheese
3 cups cooked and shredded chicken
1/2 cup chopped onions
Parmesan cheese

Blanch and drain asparagus; set aside.

Cook each tortilla in a large oiled skillet to soften. Set aside to cool and drain.

In saucepan, melt butter. Blend in flour and add chicken broth. Cook until thick and bubbly, stirring constantly. Add sour cream and taco sauce. Heat thoroughly.

Mix together 2 cups jack cheese, chicken, onion, and asparagus. Divide mixture evenly among tortillas; top each with 3 tablespoons sauce and roll. Place seam-side down in 9 x 13-inch dish. Sprinkle with remaining jack cheese, then cover with a layer of Parmesan cheese and the remaining sauce. Bake at 425°F for 25 minutes.

Serves 6

Asparagus Wild Rice Luncheon Dish

¾ cup uncooked wild rice
2 ¼ cups water
¼ tsp. salt
¾ lb. fresh asparagus cut into ¼-inch
   pieces, reserving tips
6 oz. Italian fontina cheese, diced into
   ¼-inch pieces
4 eggs
2 Tbsp. soy sauce
1 tsp. each dried thyme and basil
¼ tsp. pepper
2 Tbsp. minced fresh Italian parsley
½ cup plus 3 Tbsp. toasted wheat germ
1 Tbsp. melted butter or margarine
1 large carrot cut into thin strips for garnish (optional)
Fresh parsley sprigs for garnish (optional)

Rinse wild rice. Bring water and salt to a rapid
boil in a medium saucepan; add wild rice.
Cover pan and cook for 1 to 1¼ hours over
low heat until all liquid is absorbed and rice is
done. Set aside to cool.

Preheat oven to 325°F.

Add asparagus pieces and cheese to cooled rice.

Beat eggs lightly with soy sauce, thyme, basil, and pepper in a small bowl. Add to rice mixture along with minced parsley and ½ cup wheat germ. Place mixture in a well buttered 6 x 10 x 2-inch baking dish, patting down gently to level. Mix the remaining wheat germ with the melted butter. Distribute over top of casserole.

Bake for 40 minutes, until golden brown. Let stand 5 minutes.

To serve, cut into 6 equal portions and garnish with blanched asparagus tips, carrots, and parsley sprigs.

Serves 6

Brazilian Blades of 'Gras

4 Tbsp. butter or margarine
1 lb. flank steak, cut into 1-inch cubes
2 medium red onions, chopped
1 tsp. minced garlic
6 cups diced asparagus
2 lbs. fresh mushrooms, sliced
¾ cup red wine
1 Tbsp. red wine vinegar
8 oz. canned tomato sauce
Salt and pepper to taste
3 cups sour cream

In large skillet melt butter. Add meat, onions, and garlic, and sauté at medium-high heat for 5-6 minutes or until meat is browned. Add asparagus and mushrooms; cook until asparagus is tender but crisp. Add wine, vinegar, tomato sauce, salt, and pepper. Cook until heated through. Just before serving, add the sour cream and heat—do not boil.

Serve over noodles or steamed rice.

Serves 6

California Asparagus Commission Scallopsparagus Stir-fry

- ¾ cup chicken broth
- 1 Tbsp. cornstarch
- 1 tsp. soy sauce
- ¾ lb. sea scallops cut in half
- 1 cup sliced button or oyster mushrooms
- 1 clove garlic finely chopped
- 1 tsp. sesame oil
- ¾ lb. cooked fresh asparagus cut into 2-inch pieces
- 1 cup cherry tomato halves
- 2-3 thin green onions sliced diagonally
- Pepper to taste
- 2 cups hot cooked rice

Combine chicken broth, cornstarch, and soy sauce; set aside.

Stir-fry scallops, mushrooms, and garlic in oil about 4 minutes. Stir in cornstarch mixture. Cook, stirring until sauce thickens. Add drained asparagus, tomatoes, green onions, and pepper; heat thoroughly. Serve over rice.

Serves 4

Delicious Delta
Asparagus Flan

1 Tbsp. unsalted butter
2 Tbsp. minced onion
3 Tbsp. each minced green bell pepper and minced canned mild green chilies
1-2 Tbsp. minced canned hot jalapeno peppers
3 cups asparagus cut into 1-inch pieces
1 1/2 Tbsp. flour
1/2 cup milk
1 cup heavy whipping cream
8 eggs
1 tsp. salt
1/8 tsp. pepper
1/4 tsp. nutmeg
Pinch of ground allspice
2 cups grated Monterey jack cheese

Preheat oven to 350°F.

Melt the butter in a large skillet over medium-low heat. Add the onion and bell pepper, cooking 5 minutes. Raise the heat to medium and add the chilies, jalapeño peppers, and asparagus. Cook uncovered about 10 minutes, stirring often. Remove from heat and set aside.

Blend flour, milk and cream together until smooth. In a separate, large bowl beat the eggs until light. Add asparagus mixture, cream mixture, salt, pepper, nutmeg, allspice, and cheese; mix well. Pour into a 1½ quart shallow soufflé dish. Place the dish in a roasting pan with boiling water to reach half way up the sides of the dish. Place pan in the oven and bake for 1 hour until flan is firm. Let stand 15 minutes before serving. This dish may also be served chilled.

Serves 8

Asparagus Ravioli

DOUGH

4 cups Lapina flour
¼ cup olive oil
1 egg

FILLING

6 oz. ground veal
8 asparagus spears, finely ground
1 ground small yellow onion
3 cloves garlic, ground
2 sprigs parsley, ground
2 Tbsp. oil
1½ oz. Romano cheese
⅓ cup cooked rice
1 egg
¼ tsp. each cinnamon and Italian
    seasoning
Salt and pepper to taste

Mix dough ingredients together in large bowl. Dough should be slightly sticky—do not overknead.

Mix together veal, asparagus, onion, garlic, and parsley. Sauté in oil; cool. Add cheese, rice, egg, cinnamon, seasoning, salt and pepper. Set aside.

Make ravioli following any standard recipe.

Ravioli are done when they float to the surface after being dropped in a pot of boiling water.

Ravioli may be served in melted butter or with a favorite sauce.

As pararitos

¾ lb. skinless, boneless chicken
   breasts, cut into short, thin
   strips
2-3 cloves garlic, minced
2 Tbsp. bacon drippings
1½ cups picante sauce
1 17-oz. can black beans,
   undrained
1 large green bell pepper, chopped
1 tsp. ground cumin
Salt and pepper to taste
½ cup sliced green onions
4 slices bacon, cooked and
   crumbled
12 flour tortillas
1½ lbs. asparagus, blanched
1-1½ cups (or more) shredded
   Monterey Jack cheese
Garnishes of chopped tomatoes
   and sour cream (optional)

Cook chicken and garlic in bacon drippings until chicken is done. Stir in ½ cup picante sauce, beans, bell pepper, cumin, salt, and pepper. Simmer 7-8 minutes until thickened, stirring occasionally. Stir in green onions and bacon.

Spoon bean mixture down center of each tortilla. Add 2-3 asparagus stalks; top with cheese. Roll up tortillas and place seam side down in lightly greased 9 x 13-inch baking dish. Spoon remaining sauce over top. Bake at 350°F for 15 minutes. Top with remaining cheese, then return to oven until cheese melts.

Garnish as desired and serve with additional sauce.

Serves 6

Asparagus Stick'ers

1 lb. asparagus tips
1 Tbsp. fresh cilantro
½ lb. mild or hot Italian sausage
3 Tbsp. soy sauce
2 Tbsp. dry sherry
1 Tbsp. each sesame oil and cornstarch
2 oz. (½ 4 oz. can) bamboo shoots
1 egg
1 pkg. round pot sticker wrappers
Vegetable oil for frying
1 cup chicken broth

Place asparagus and cilantro in food processor; chop very fine. Add sausage and blend well. Add soy sauce, sherry, sesame oil, cornstarch, bamboo shoots, and egg, and process until well mixed.

Place 1 heaping tsp. of mixture in middle of a pot sticker wrapper and lightly moisten entire edge with water. Lift both sides of skin and pinch together to seal. Repeat procedure until all ingredients are used.

Heat oil in a nonstick skillet with a
tight fitting lid over medium high heat.
Use enough oil to generously coat bottom
of pan. Arrange pot stickers in pan, pleated
sides up. Cook until edges begin to brown.
Add 1/4 cup chicken broth carefully and immediately cover pan. Reduce heat to medium and
cook 6-8 minutes until stickers have swollen
and liquid is nearly evaporated. Remove lid
and increase heat to medium high. Cook until
liquid boils away and stickers begin to sizzle
in remaining oil (add more oil if necessary).
Continue cooking until bottoms become crisp
and golden brown. Repeat procedure until all
stickers are cooked.

When serving, offer soy sauce, vinegar, and
chili oil as dipping sauces.

Serves 4

Martin Yan's Asparagus with Sweet Sesame Dressing

1 lb. asparagus cut into 2-inch diagonal
  slices and cooked until tender but crisp

DRESSING

2 Tbsp. packed light brown sugar
1 Tbsp. each sesame oil, soy sauce, rice
  vinegar, sesame paste, and mirin
  (Japanese sweet rice wine)
1 Tbsp. toasted sesame seeds

Combine dressing ingredients in a small sauce-pan. Heat over medium heat until sugar and sesame paste are dissolved. Simmer, stirring constantly, until slightly thickened, about 1-2 minutes.

Arrange asparagus on a serving platter. Spoon dressing over asparagus, sprinkle with sesame seeds and serve immediately.

Serves 4

Roasted Asparagus

2 lbs. asparagus
1 Tbsp. extra virgin olive oil
$1/2$ tsp. salt
$1/8$ tsp. pepper
8 lemon wedges for garnish

Preheat oven to 425°F.

Put asparagus in 10 x 15-inch jelly-roll pan. Drizzle asparagus with oil and sprinkle with salt and pepper. Turn until evenly coated, then arrange in a single layer.

Roast 10-15 minutes until tender and tips begin to brown. Serve immediately garnished with lemon wedges.

Variation: Add $1/2$ tsp. dried thyme or 1 tsp. chopped fresh thyme before roasting.

Asparagus Lasagna

1-2 lbs. fresh or frozen asparagus
 cut into 1-inch pieces
3 Tbsp. butter
2 green onions, chopped
12 oz. fresh mushrooms, chopped
1/4 cup flour
1 tsp. salt
1/4 tsp. cayenne pepper
2 1/2 cups milk
8 oz. lasagna noodles, cooked
2 cups cottage cheese
2 cups shredded jack cheese
 (or more)
1/2-1 cup grated Parmesan cheese
 (or more)
Black pepper to taste (optional)

Cook asparagus and drain; let cool.

Preheat oven to 325°F.

Melt butter in medium size saucepan. Add onions and mushrooms and cook over medium heat about 5 minutes. Blend in flour, salt, and cayenne pepper. Gradually stir in milk. Cook sauce until thickened for additional 5 minutes.

Spread 1/2 cup sauce in greased 9 x 13-inch baking dish. Layer noodles (season with pepper for more spicy flavor), asparagus, cottage cheese, jack cheese, 1/3 remaining sauce, and Parmesan cheese. Repeat to make three layers.

Bake for 45 minutes. Let stand 20 minutes before cutting to serve.

Serves 12

Asparagus Bruschetta

1 cup ricotta cheese
2 Tbsp. oil-packed sundried tomatoes,
  drained and finely chopped
1 Tbsp. each diced black olives and
  chopped parsley
1 green onion, minced
1/4 tsp. each grated lemon peel and
  lemon pepper
1 loaf crusty Italian or French bread
1 lb. cooked asparagus cut into
  4-inch pieces
1/2 cup shredded mozzarella cheese
1 Tbsp. each olive oil, balsamic vinegar, and snipped basil leaves
1 clove garlic, pressed
Cherry tomatoes for garnish

Preheat oven to 400°F.

Combine ricotta, sundried tomatoes, olives, parsley, onion, lemon peel, and lemon pepper. Mix well and set aside.

Cut the bread in thirds horizontally. Trim crusts so the bread sits level. Cut each piece in half crosswise to make 6 pieces. Spread the cut sides of the bread with the ricotta mixture, arrange asparagus on top of it, then sprinkle with mozzarella.

Place on a baking sheet. Bake for 5 minutes.

Combine oil, vinegar, basil, and garlic. Drizzle over the bruschetta. Garnish and serve.

Serves 6

Chicken Asparagus Bake

      5 Tbsp. each butter and flour
      1½ cups chicken broth
      6-oz. can mushrooms, drained
      Dash pepper
      2 large chicken breasts, cooked
        and sliced
      1 lb. cooked fresh asparagus spears
      ¼ cup dry bread crumbs
      2 Tbsp. each snipped parsley, toasted
        slivered almonds, and melted butter

Preheat oven to 375°F.

Melt butter; blend in flour. Add chicken broth;
cook and stir until mixture is thickened. Add
mushrooms and pepper.

Place chicken in bottom of 6 x 10 x 1½-inch
baking dish. Drizzle with half the mushroom
sauce. Arrange asparagus spears over sauce,
then pour on remaining sauce.

Combine crumbs, parsley, almonds, and melted
butter. Sprinkle over casserole. Bake 20 minutes.

Serves 4

'Gras Quiche Italienne

1 cup shredded swiss cheese
1 9-inch baked pie shell
1/2 lb. Italian sausage, casings
removed, cut into 1/2-inch pieces
1/2 lb. asparagus trimmed to 5 inches,
then sliced diagonally
1/4 cup finely chopped onion
4 eggs, slightly beaten
1 1/2 cups milk or light cream
2 Tbsp. fresh minced parsley
1/4 tsp. salt

Preheat oven to 325°F.

Sprinkle 1/2 cup cheese in bottom of pie shell. Brown sausage in skillet; drain and discard fat. Remove sausage from pan and set aside.

Sauté asparagus in skillet over low to medium heat until tender. Add onion and sauté 2 minutes longer. Return sausage to skillet. Stir while cooking for 2 minutes more. Spoon into pie shell.

Combine eggs, milk, parsley, and salt. Pour into shell. Sprinkle with remaining 1/2 cup cheese. Bake for 45-50 minutes.

Serves 6

You're Kidding! There's Asparagus in Here?

All recipes require cleaned and trimmed asparagus.

Kitty's Asparagus Margarita

1 lb. fresh asparagus, blanched
    and chopped
10 oz. margarita mix
6 oz. tequila
8 oz. crushed ice
1 lime, quartered
1 tsp. seasoned salt
6 spears asparagus, blanched

Place chopped asparagus, margarita mix, tequila, and crushed ice into blender; blend until smooth.

Rub top rim of 6 glasses with lime. Place salt on plate and dip glasses to cover rims with salt. Garnish with asparagus spear and serve.

Serves 6

No Guilt Asparagus Guacamole

4 cups fresh or frozen asparagus, cut
  into 1-inch pieces
1 clove garlic, minced
2 tsp. lime juice
1/4 cup canned, chopped green chilies
1/2 tsp. each salt and cumin
2 Tbsp. finely chopped onion
1/2 cup chopped, seeded tomato

Cook asparagus in small amount of water until tender. Drain well and cool thoroughly.

In food processor or blender, process asparagus, garlic, lime juice, chilies, salt, and cumin until mixture is smooth, about 30 seconds.

Remove mixture from food processor and stir in onion and tomato. Chill thoroughly before serving with tortilla chips, cut vegetables, chicken, or seafood.

Yield: 2 cups

This recipe was shared by *The Michigan Asparagus Advisory Board*

Asparagus Italian Focaccia Bread

4½ cups flour
2 tsp. salt
1 pkg. dry yeast
1½ tsp. sugar
1¾ cups warm water
7 Tbsp. extra virgin olive oil
1 lb. asparagus, thinly sliced on the diagonal
1 medium onion, chopped

Combine 4 cups flour, salt, yeast, and sugar in bowl or food processor. Mix well. Add water and 2 Tbsp. oil; mix well. Let dough rise 1½-2 hours.

In fry pan, add 1 Tbsp. oil and sautè asparagus and onion about 15 minutes. Cool.

Oil hands and a 11 x 15-inch cookie pan with 1 Tbsp. oil. Punch dough down, then add asparagus mixture and remaining flour. Let dough rise 1½-2 hours until dough is approximately 2-inches thick. Brush remaining oil over the top of the focaccia, then sprinkle lightly with salt. Poke holes with fingers into the loaf.

Bake at 350°F in preheated oven for 45 minutes or until lightly browned. Cool for ½ hour before serving.

Asparagus Salsa

1 red bell pepper, minced
1 green bell pepper, minced
1 13-oz. can pre-sliced, peeled
  tomatoes
4 Roma tomatoes, minced
1 Tbsp. Tabasco sauce
Salt to taste
Chopped green onions to taste
1 cup minced fresh asparagus

In a bowl, mix all ingredients well. Refrigerate at least 1 hour, then season to taste. Serve with chips.

Yield: Approximately 5-6 cups

Asparaberry Jelly

4 pints strawberries, crushed
2 lbs. asparagus, ground
1/2 cup water
1/4 cup lemon juice
1 pkg. pectin
4 1/2 cups sugar

Bring strawberries to a boil. Measure out 1 1/2 cups of the juice and set aside. Bring asparagus and water to a boil; simmer until asparagus is tender. Measure out 1 1/2 cups asparagus juice. Combine juices with lemon and pectin. Mix well and bring to a boil. Add sugar all at once, bringing to another boil. Stir constantly. Boil hard for 2 minutes. Skim, then fill hot sterilized jars. Leave 1/8 inch headspace. Clean rims. Process 5 minutes in water bath. (See page 94.)

Yield: 3-4 pints

Pickled Asparagus

8 lbs. asparagus spears, trimmed to fit
  8 pint jars
8 cloves garlic
1 quart each vinegar and water
4 Tbsp. salt
1 Tbsp. whole, mixed pickling spice

Blanch asparagus spears 1 minute. Cool in ice water.

Pack clean, hot pint jars with 1 clove garlic and asparagus.

Heat vinegar, water, salt, and spice to simmering, then pour over asparagus. Leave ½ inch headspace. Wipe rim of jar with clean cloth.

Process in a water bath for 15 minutes at 170°F. (See page 94.)

Variations: add fresh or dried dillweed along with garlic. If dill is used, pickling spice is optional. Or, add 6 black peppercorns, 1 dried red chili pepper, and 1 tsp. dried dill seed or fresh dill to each jar.

Yield: 8 pints

Delightfully Tart
Spread

4 cups chopped kiwi
2 cups chopped pears
1 lb. asparagus, chopped
2-3 cups sugar (adjust to taste)
⅛ tsp. nutmeg

Place all ingredients in pan. Cook on low temperature to reduce. When fruit is soft, use potato masher or mixer to smooth texture. Fill jars and refrigerate.

Yield 2-3 pints

Technicolor Asparagus Pickles

    2 thinly sliced onions
    4 cloves garlic
    4 Tbsp. pickling spice
    4 dried red peppers (optional)
    2 cups each cider vinegar and water
    2 Tbsp. salt
    3 Tbsp. sugar
    4 lbs. asparagus trimmed to fit the jars
    2 red bell peppers cut into strips

Divide onions among 4 pint jars. Place 1 clove garlic, 1 Tbsp. pickling spice, and 1 dried pepper in each jar.

Bring vinegar, water, salt, and sugar to a boil in a sauce pan.

Pack jars with asparagus and bell peppers. Cover with hot liquid. Leave ½ inch headspace. Clean rims.

Process 20 minutes in water bath. (See page 94.)

Yield: 4 pints

Sweet Asparagus Pickles

4 lbs. asparagus trimmed to fit
   4 pint jars
2 cups vinegar
1 cup water
½ cup sugar
1 tsp. whole allspice
6 whole cloves
3 inches stick cinnamon

Cover asparagus with boiling water; cook
3 minutes, drain. Pack lengthwise into hot
pint jars, leaving ½-inch head space. In a
saucepan combine vinegar, water, and sugar.
Tie allspice, cloves, and cinnamon in a cheese-
cloth bag. Add spice bag to pickling liquid.
Simmer 15 minutes. Cover asparagus with hot
pickling liquid leaving ½-inch head space.
Process in boiling water bath 10 minutes at
170°F. (See page 94.)

Yield: 4 pints

Bread and Butter Asparagus Pickles

⅓ cup salt
3 cups distilled vinegar
2 cups sugar
2 Tbsp. mustard seed
2 tsp. each turmeric and celery seed
1 tsp. each ground ginger and peppercorns
5 lbs. asparagus, cut into 1-inch pieces
10 small onions, thinly sliced

Bring salt, vinegar, sugar, mustard, turmeric, and celery seeds to boil with ginger and peppercorns. Add asparagus and onions and bring to another boil. Pack hot into hot jars, leaving ¼-inch head space. Remove air bubbles. Process 15 minutes in boiling water bath. (See page 94.)

Yield: 4-5 pints

Waste Not, Want Not
Asparagus Cake

CAKE

3 cups peeled white ends of asparagus
1 piece peeled fresh ginger (size of
   large walnut)
Zest of 1 lemon
Zest of 1 orange
1 cup chopped walnuts, drenched in
   flour
2 cups each sugar and flour
1 tsp. each baking soda, cinnamon,
   nutmeg, and salt
1½ cups vegetable oil
4 eggs

SPICED WHIPPED
CREAM TOPPING

1 cup whipping cream
1 Tbsp. sugar
½ tsp. nutmeg
2 Tbsp. crystallized candied ginger,
   finely chopped

Preheat oven to 325°F.

Grind asparagus and ginger with coarse
blade of meat grinder. Add zests and walnuts.
Set aside.

In a separate bowl, mix together the sugar,
flour, baking soda, cinnamon, nutmeg, and
salt. Add oil and eggs; beat until well mixed.
Fold in asparagus mixture. Pour into a greased
and floured 9 x 13-inch pan.

Bake for 1 hour

Topping: Whip the cream, adding sugar a little
at a time. Fold in the nutmeg and ginger.
Serve cake warm, with spiced whipped cream.

Serves 10

Asparagus Poppy Seed Loaf

STREUSEL TOPPING

¼ cup each sugar and lightly
  packed brown sugar
1 Tbsp. flour
2 Tbsp. butter, room temperature

LOAF

2 cups flour
½ tsp. each salt and baking soda
¾ tsp. baking powder
¼ cup butter, room temperature
2 eggs, room temperature
¾ cup sugar
1 cup sour cream
1½ tsp. vanilla extract
¼ cup each cream sherry and
  poppy seeds
¾ cup finely chopped fresh
  asparagus

Preheat oven to 375°F.

Combine all streusel ingredients and mix until crumbly. Set aside.

Sift together flour, salt, baking soda, and baking powder. Set aside.

In a large mixing bowl, beat the butter, eggs, and sugar until well blended. Mix in sour cream, vanilla, cream sherry, and poppy seeds until well mixed. Fold in sifted ingredients and asparagus. Pour batter into a 5 x 9-inch loaf pan that has been lightly buttered and floured. Sprinkle evenly with streusel topping mixture.

Bake for 55-60 minutes or until a toothpick inserted into center comes out clean.

Yield: 1 loaf

Asparagus Sherry Cake

3 cups sifted flour
2 tsp. cinnamon
1 1/4 tsp. salt
1 tsp. baking powder
1 1/2 tsp. baking soda
1 cup oil
2 cups sugar
3 eggs
1 tsp. each vanilla and lemon peel
4 Tbsp. cooking sherry
2 cups finely diced asparagus
1 1/2 cups chopped pecans
1 cup chopped fresh cranberries
1/4 cup powdered sugar
1 Tbsp. milk

Preheat oven to 325°F.

Combine flour, cinnamon, salt, baking powder, and baking soda. Mix well; set aside.

Beat together oil, sugar, and eggs. Add vanilla, lemon peel, sherry, and asparagus. Fold in dry ingredients; mix well. Add pecans and cranberries.

Pour batter into 10-inch greased and floured tube pan.

Bake for one hour and 15 minutes. Cool before removing from pan.

Combine powdered sugar with milk to make frosting. Place cake on cake plate and decorate with frosting.

Serves 12

Asparabread

3 cups flour
1 tsp. each salt and baking soda
1/4 tsp. baking powder
1 cup oil
3 eggs
2 cups each sugar and grated
  asparagus
2 tsp. vanilla
1/2 tsp. each nutmeg and allspice
3 tsp. cinnamon
1/2 cup chopped nuts

Preheat oven to 350°F.

Sift together flour, salt, baking soda and baking powder. Set aside. Beat together oil, eggs, sugar, asparagus, and vanilla: add to dry ingredients. Add spices and nuts; mix by hand until ingredients are moistened. Divide batter into 2 greased 5 x 9-inch loaf pans.

Bake for 1 hour or until toothpick inserted in center of loaf comes out clean.

Variation: Substitute 1 cup crushed drained pineapple for 1 cup grated asparagus.

Yield: 2 loaves

The End

Water Bath Process

1. Prepare lids according to manufacturer's instructions.

2. Fill clean hot jars with asparagus to within 1/2 inch of the rim.

3. Cover the asparagus with hot liquid or brine. Leave 1/2 inch headspace (the distance between the contents and the rim of the jar.)

4. Remove air bubbles by running a plastic knife or spatula between the asparagus and the jar.

5. Clean rim and threads of the jar.

6. Place heated lid on jar and secure with a hot ring band. Screw the band down so that it is hand tight.

7. Place jars in a water bath or deep kettle with a rack. The water bath should be about half full before loading. Water should be very hot but not boiling. Add enough water to cover the tops of the jars by at least 1 inch.

8. Begin to time when the water bath temperature reaches 180°F.

9. As you take the jar from the water bath, hold level, but do not disturb the seal. Leave the ring bands on the jars until thoroughly cooled.

10. Place the hot jars, well separated, on a rack or folded towel away from drafts or cool surfaces. Remove rings to store jars.

Conversion Chart

LIQUID
1 Tbsp = 15 ml
1/2 cup = 4 fl oz = 125 ml
1 cup = 8 fl oz = 250 ml

DRY
1/4 cup = 4 Tbsp = 2 oz = 60 g
1 cup = 1/2 pound = 8 oz = 250 g

FLOUR
1/2 cup = 60 g
1 cup = 4 oz = 125 g

TEMPERATURE
400°F = 200° C = gas mark 6
375°F = 190° C = gas mark 5
350°F = 175° C = gas mark 4

MISCELLANEOUS
2 Tbsp butter = 1 oz = 30 g
1 inch = 2.5 cm
all-purpose flour = plain flour
baking soda = bicarbonate of soda
heavy cream = double cream
sugar = caster sugar